The Life and Work of...

Vincent van Gogh

Sean Connolly

Heinemann Library
Chicago, Illinois

© 2000 Reed Educational & Professional Publishing
Published by Heinemann Library,
an imprint of Reed Educational & Professional Publishing,
100 N. LaSalle, Suite 1010
Chicago, IL 60602

Customer Service 1-888-454-2279
Visit our website at www.heinemannlibrary.com

Text designed by Celia Floyd
Illustrations by Sam Thompson
Printed in Hong Kong,China

05 04 03 02 01
10 9 8 7 6 5 4 3 2

Library of Congress Cataloging-in-Publication Data
Connolly, Sean, 1956-
     Vincent Van Gogh / Sean Connolly.
        p. cm. – (The life and work of--) (Heinemann profiles)
     Includes bibliographical references and index.
     Summary: Introduces the life and work of Vincent Van Gogh, discussing his early years, life in Holland, London, Paris, and southern France, and development as a painter.
     ISBN 1-57572-958-X (lib. binding)
     1. Gogh, Vincent van, 1853-1890 Juvenile literature. 2. Painters —Netherlands Biography Juvenile literature. [1. Gogh, Vincent van, 1853-1890. 2. Artists. 3. Painting, Dutch. 4. Art appreciation.]
     I. Title. II. Series. III. Series: Heinemann profiles.
     ND653.G7C56 1999
     759.9492—dc21
     [B]   99-14547
                                                                         CIP

Acknowledgments
The Publishers would like to thank the following for permission to reproduce photographs:
Page 5, Vincent van Gogh, *Self Portrait with Shaven Head*, Credit: The Bridgeman Art Library/Fogg Art Museum. Page 7, Vincent van Gogh, *Milk Jug*, Credit: Stichting Kröller-Müller Museum. Page 8, Portrait Photo of van Gogh's uncle, founder of The Hague branch of Goupil & Co., Credit: AKG. Page 9, Vincent van Gogh, *Noon, or The Siesta, after Millet*, Credit: The Bridgeman Art Library. Page 10, Coal mining in Belgium, Credit: AKG. Page 11, Vincent van Gogh, *Miners' Wives*, Credit: The Bridgeman Art Library. Page 13, Vincent van Gogh, *Portrait of Theodore van Gogh*, Credit: The Bridgeman Art Library. Page 15, Vincent van Gogh, *Two Peasants Planting Potatoes*, Credit: The Bridgeman Art Library. Page 17, Vincent van Gogh, *The Allotments*, Credit: The Bridgeman Art Library. Page 19, Vincent van Gogh, *Portrait of the Artist*, Credit: Image Select. Page 21, Vincent van Gogh, *The Night Café*, Credit: B & U International. Page 23, Vincent van Gogh, *Self-Portrait with Bandaged Ear*, Credit: Exley/Rosenthal. Page 25, Vincent van Gogh, *The Asylum Garden at Arles*, Credit: The Bridgeman Art Library/Oskar Reinhart Collection. Page 27, Vincent van Gogh, *Wheatfield with Cypresses*, Credit: AKG. Page 29, Vincent van Gogh, *Crows over Wheatfield*, Credit: Exley/Rosenthal.
Cover photograph reproduced with permission of Bridgeman Art Library.
Our thanks to Paul Flux for his comments in the preparation of this book.
Every effort has been made to contact copyright holders of any material reproduced in this book. Any omissions will be rectified in subsequent printings if notice is given to the Publisher.

Some words in this book are in bold, **like this.** You can find out what they mean by looking in the glossary.

Contents

Who Was Vincent van Gogh?

Vincent van Gogh was a **Dutch** artist. He made many great paintings during his short, sad life. Vincent's art was not well-known until after he died.

4

This **self-portrait** shows Vincent at age 35—about two years before he died. He was very unhappy.

Early Years

Vincent van Gogh was born in a small village in Holland on March 30, 1853. His father was a **pastor**. His younger brother Theo was one of his few friends.

Vincent was good at drawing. He made this **sketch** when he was nine years old. It shows how well he could draw what he saw around him.

Different Jobs

Vincent left school when he was 15 years old. He worked in many different jobs. His uncle got him a job with an **art dealer** in London. This is a photograph of Vincent's uncle.

In his job, Vincent saw paintings by many great artists. He liked a French artist named Millet. Vincent made this painting. It looks like a painting by Millet.

Among the Poor

Vincent found his work hard. He lost his job. He wanted a big change in his life. When he was 25 years old, he began to **study** to be a **preacher** in a **mining** area of Belgium.

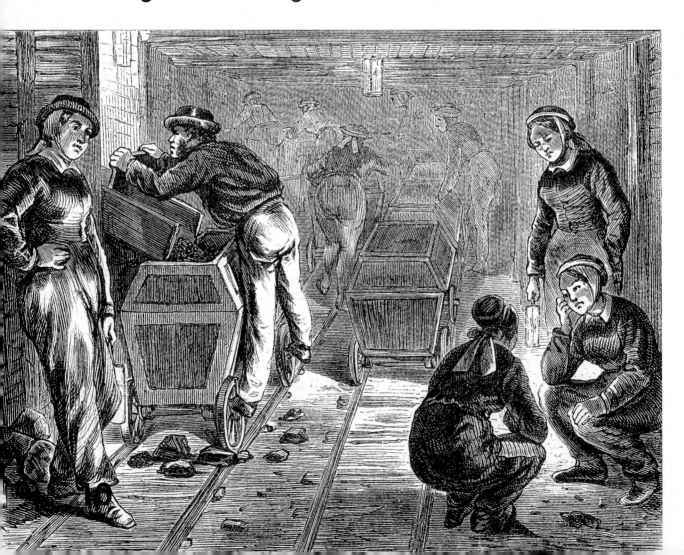

Vincent soon left these studies. He went to preach to **miners**. He gave his things to these poor people. This painting shows some of the miners' wives.

Drawing His Feelings

When Vincent was 27 years old, he gave up
preaching and **studied** art. He went to join his
family. Vincent's parents had moved to Etten,
a small **Dutch** village.

Vincent argued with his father and other people.

Vincent shows his father's serious face in this **sketch**.

Sadness

Things got worse between Vincent and his family. Vincent left home. He moved around Holland and Belgium. His father died in 1885. Vincent felt bad.

14

Vincent felt happier when he was able to draw and paint. He loved showing ordinary people at work.

Moving to Paris

In 1886, Vincent went to Paris to live with his brother Theo. He saw how some artists—called the **Impressionists**—worked outside. Their paintings were full of light and color.

Vincent also began to work outside. This is a painting of gardens in a village near Paris. Vincent used quick **brush strokes** to make the picture.

Bright Colors

Theo helped Vincent meet other artists in Paris.
Vincent began to paint with bright colors. The
colors showed Vincent's moods and feelings.

In this **self-portrait,** Vincent added the bold colors quickly and thickly. His face seems to look out through a crust of colors.

Moving South

In 1888, Vincent moved to southern France. A painter named Paul Gauguin joined him in the town of Arles. Both artists loved the colorful countryside there.

Everything about southern France seemed exciting to Vincent. This lively painting of a café at night shows these feelings.

Signs of Trouble

Vincent often became angry or sad. Paul Gauguin left after an argument. Vincent felt bad almost all of the time. In December of 1888, Vincent cut off part of his ear. He was taken to a hospital.

22

Vincent felt calm again as the ear got better.
He began to paint again. This **self-portrait**
shows the bandage on his ear.

23

Illness

The peace did not last long. Vincent began to hear strange voices in his head. In May of 1889, he entered an **asylum** to be looked after.

Vincent felt better at the asylum. He painted there. The doctors thought that was good for Vincent. This painting shows the peaceful garden at the asylum.

Burst of Joy

Vincent spent a year in the **asylum**. He painted more than 150 pictures. He sent some to Paris but could not sell them.

Vincent's work was better than ever. The colors and curving lines of this painting seem full of his excitement.

Vincent's Last Days

Vincent went to live near Paris. He still painted, but he became sad again. Theo asked a kind doctor to help Vincent. Even the doctor could not help him.

This is one of the last of Vincent's 800 paintings.
He was sad and afraid when he painted it. In July,
1890, Vincent killed himself.

Timeline

1853   Vincent van Gogh is born, March 30

1865   American Civil War ends

1869–76   Vincent works for the **art dealer** Goupil in Holland, London, and Paris

1870–71   War between France and Germany

1876   The telephone is invented

1877–81   Vincent trains to be a **preacher** and then lives with Belgian **miners**

1881   Vincent joins his family, quarrels with his father, travels around Holland and Belgium

1885   Vincent's father dies

1886   Vincent goes to live with his brother Theo in Paris

1888   In December, Vincent cuts off part of his ear

1889   Vincent goes into an **asylum** for a year

1890   Vincent dies, July 29

Glossary

art dealer   person who sells paintings

asylum   hospital for people with mental illnesses

brush stroke   mark left by an artist's paint brush

Dutch   someone or something from Holland

Impressionists   group of artists who painted outside to make colorful pictures

miner   someone who digs for coal underground

mining   digging coal from under the ground

pastor   someone who leads a local church

preacher   person who tells others about religion

self-portrait   drawing or painting of a person done by that person

sketch   drawing

study   learn about a subject

Index

More Books to Read

Crispino, Enrica. *Van Gogh*. Peter Bedrick Books, 1996.

Lucas, Eileen. *Vincent Van Gogh*. Lerner Publishing Group, 1997.

Venezia, Mike. *Van Gogh*. Danbury, Conn. : Children's Press, 1988.
An older reader can help you with these books.

More Artwork to See

Le Moulin de la Galette, 1887. Museum of Art, Pittsburgh, Penn.

The Night Café, 1888. Yale University Gallery, New Haven, Conn.

Self-Portrait, 1889. National Gallery of Art, Washington, D.C.